Marie Curie

The Woman Behind Radioactivity

by Nancy Dickmann

PEBBLE
a capstone imprint

Little Explorer is published by Pebble,
1710 Roe Crest Drive, North Mankato, Minnesota 56003
www.capstonepub.com

Library of Congress Cataloging-in-Publication Data
Names: Dickmann, Nancy, author.
Title: Marie Curie: the woman behind radioactivity / by Nancy Dickmann.
Description: North Mankato, Minnesota : Pebble, [2020] | Series: Smithsonian little explorer. little
inventor | Audience: Ages: 6–8. | Audience: Grades: K–3. | Includes bibliographical references.
Identifiers: LCCN 2018061609| ISBN 9781977109767 (hardcover) | ISBN 9781977110596 (pbk.) |
ISBN 9781977109866 (ebook pdf) Subjects: LCSH: Curie, Marie, 1867–1934—Juvenile literature. |
Women chemists—France—Biography—Juvenile literature. | Scientists—France—Biography—Juvenile
literature. | Radioactivity—Juvenile literature. | Nobel Prize winners—Biography—Juvenile literature.
Classification: LCC QD22.C8 D53 2020 | DDC 540.92 [B]—dc22
LC record available at https://lccn.loc.gov/2018061609

Editorial Credits
Erika L. Shores, editor; Kayla Rossow, designer; Svetlana Zhurkin, media researcher;
Tori Abraham, production specialist

Our very special thanks to Emma Grahn, Spark!Lab Manager, Lemelson Center for the Study of
Invention and Innovation at the National Museum of American History. Capstone would also like to
thank Kealy Gordon, Product Development Manager, and the following at Smithsonian Enterprises:
Ellen Nanney, Licensing Manager; Brigid Ferraro, Vice President, Education and Consumer Products;
and Carol LeBlanc, Senior Vice President, Education and Consumer Products.

Image Credits
Alamy: Lebrecht Music & Arts, 7; Getty Image: Hulton Archive, cover; Library of Congress, 27; Mary
Evans Picture Library, 23; Newscom: Album/Prisma, 13 (top), Everett Collection, 19, Heritage Images/
Fine Art Images, 6, Heritage Images/The Print Collector, 13 (bottom), MAXPPP/IP3 Press/Marlene
Awaad, 29, World History Archive, 9 (top), 11, 17, 20, 25, 26; North Wind Picture Archives, 12;
Shutterstock: Bjoern Wylezich, 14, Everett Historical, 5, 10, Humdan, 15 (bottom), Mark Kostich, 4,
Morphart Creation, 9 (bottom), trabantos, 28; SuperStock: DeAgostini, 15 (top)

Design Elements by Shutterstock

All internet sites appearing in back matter were available and accurate when this book
was sent to press.

Printed in the United States of America.
PA70

TABLE OF CONTENTS

INTRODUCTION

Modern medicine is amazing! Doctors can heal bodies. They can treat diseases such as cancer. They often make use of a treatment called radiation. It is based on a property called radioactivity.

Radiation treatment damages cancer cells. It stops the cancer from growing.

Why do we use radioactivity in medicine? It's all thanks to a scientist named Marie Curie! Scientists are people who study the natural world. They ask questions. They do experiments to find the answers.

Marie Curie was one of the world's most famous scientists.

EARLY LIFE

Marie was born in Poland in 1867. Her parents were teachers, and they valued education. Marie loved learning. She worked hard at school. Her father taught her about science.

Marie's dream was to go to college. But back then in Poland, only boys were allowed. Marie didn't want to stop learning, though. She studied at a secret night school instead.

Marie at age 16

Marie's name at birth was Maria Sklodowska. She was the youngest of five children. Young Marie is seated in the middle here.

SECRET SCHOOL

Poland's government controlled who could go to college. Some teachers started their own secret university. They taught anyone who wanted to learn. This was against the law. They met in secret at people's homes.

STUDIES IN PARIS

A university in France let women study. Marie and her sister, Bronya, made a deal. They would help each other go to school. They would take turns working. First, Marie would find a job.

Marie paid for her sister to study in Paris. After her sister finished, it was Marie's turn to learn. The plan worked. In 1891 Marie moved to Paris. She studied physics, math, and chemistry.

Marie (left) with her sister, Bronya, in 1886

Marie went to school at the Sorbonne in Paris. Her sister had studied medicine there and became a doctor.

The courtyard of Sorbonne University

PIERRE CURIE

Marie did well in her studies. She was given a project studying metals. But she needed a lab. A friend introduced her to Pierre Curie. He ran a chemistry lab. He let her work there.

Pierre and Marie Curie

Marie and Pierre soon fell in love. They got married in 1895. The Curies were partners in life and science. They worked together in the lab. Marie wanted to be the first woman to earn a doctorate in science.

Pierre and Marie bought bikes for each other as wedding gifts. They rode their bikes around France on their honeymoon trip.

RADIOACTIVITY

Radiation is energy traveling through space. Light is one form of radiation. There are other types too. In 1895 a new type, called X-rays, was discovered. X-rays could travel through solid objects.

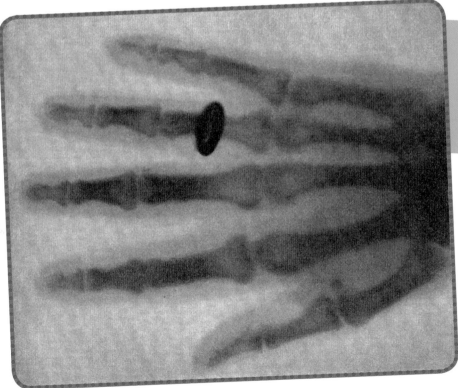

An X-ray photograph of a hand was taken in 1896 in Germany.

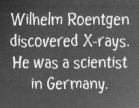

Henri Becquerel

Then, scientist Henri Becquerel found that some materials give off radiation. Their atoms are unstable. They release tiny bits of matter. They also release energy. Marie Curie invented a word for this. She called it radioactivity.

FINDING POLONIUM

Marie studied Becquerel's rays. They came from uranium. She tested a mineral that contained uranium. But it gave off too much radiation. She guessed that it held another radioactive element.

The mineral Marie tested was called pitchblende.
Today it is known as uraninite.

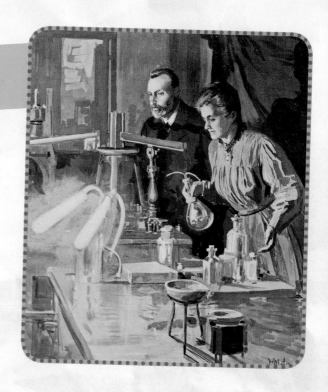

The Curies needed to find it. They used acid to break down the mineral. They removed some of its elements. What was left was very radioactive. The new element was in there. They called it polonium.

Periodic Table of the Elements

ELEMENTS

There are more than 100 different elements. Everything in the universe is made from them. Scientists keep looking for new elements.

RADIUM

The Curies found another element. They called it radium. But it was a tiny amount. It was mixed with other things. No one could see or measure it. Some scientists did not believe their discovery.

Marie tried to separate the new elements. It took years of hard work. She needed tons of pitchblende. She ground it and treated it. At last she had a speck of nearly pure radium.

"I am among those who think that science has great beauty."

—Marie Curie

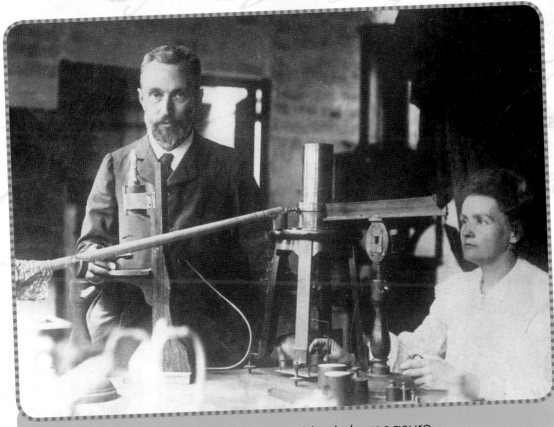

Pierre and Marie used tools to measure
the radioactivity of new elements.

ELEMENTS THE CURIES STUDIED

	Uranium	Polonium	Radium
Discovered	1789	1898	1898
Named after	Uranus	Poland	Latin for "ray"
Appearance	silvery	silvery-gray	soft, shiny, silvery

TRIUMPH AND TRAGEDY

In 1903 Marie and Pierre won the Nobel Prize in Physics. It is the world's top prize for this field of science. They shared it with Henri Becquerel. They won for their work on radioactivity.

Just three years later, Pierre died. He was killed in a road accident. He was only 46 years old. Marie had lost her husband. She had also lost her partner in the science lab.

Nobel Prizes are awarded in physics, chemistry, medicine, literature, and peace.

Pierre and Marie shared a love of science.

MAKING HER MARK

Pierre's death was shocking and sad. But Marie knew she had to go on. She became a professor. She took over Pierre's job. Pierre's father helped take care of the Curies' daughters, Irène and Eve.

Marie continued researching after Pierre's death.

Marie finally separated pure radium. She won another Nobel Prize in 1911. This time she won on her own. The prize was for discovering radium and polonium. She was the first person to win twice.

Marie was the first female professor at the Sorbonne.

WINNERS OF TWO NOBEL PRIZES

NAME	FIRST PRIZE	SECOND PRIZE
Marie Curie	1903 (Physics)	1911 (Chemistry)
Linus Pauling	1954 (Chemistry)	1962 (Peace)
John Bardeen	1956 (Physics)	1972 (Physics)
Frederick Sanger	1958 (Chemistry)	1980 (Chemistry)

USING RADIOACTIVITY

Marie didn't care about being rich or famous. She wanted to make new discoveries. She wanted her discoveries to help people. X-rays could help doctors. Radiation could be used to treat cancer.

Radiation can also be deadly. At first no one knew how dangerous it was. Even Marie did not always stay safe. Working with radioactive materials made her ill.

"I am one of those who think . . . that humanity will draw more good than evil from new discoveries."

—Marie Curie

Both Pierre and Marie had suffered from the effects of radiation. They were tired all the time. The skin on their hands was cracked and scarred.

Marie spoke with nurses about radiation treatment.

WORLD WAR I

In 1914 World War I began. Many soldiers were wounded. X-rays could help doctors find bullets. But there were few X-ray machines. They were in city hospitals, far away from the fighting.

Marie wanted to help. She helped make a special car. It had an X-ray machine inside. She trained women to use the machines. Marie learned to drive. Now she could drive an X-ray car to the battlefield.

Marie brought X-ray machines to battlefields during World War I. People called the vehicles "petite Curies" or "little Curies."

DOCTORS AT WAR

Army doctors had a hard job. They had to treat soldiers near the battlefield. They often worked in tents. They did not always have good tools. They were in danger from enemy attacks.

When the war was over, Marie went back to the lab. Her daughter Irène helped her. She was a scientist too. Marie started a new lab. It would help scientists find new ways to use radioactivity.

Irène Joliot-Curie won a Nobel Prize for chemistry in 1935.

Irène and Marie in 1925

Marie won many prizes. She gave speeches in other countries. She met famous scientist Albert Einstein and two U.S. presidents. Marie died in 1934. Her work with radioactivity may have caused her illness.

U.S. President Warren Harding and Marie on the steps of the White House in Washington, D.C.

CURIE'S LEGACY

We owe a lot to Marie Curie. She discovered two new elements. Her work helped us understand radioactivity. Now doctors can use it to help people.

Marie also broke down barriers for women. She worked hard to get an education. She showed that college was not just for boys. She proved that women could be scientists. Today there are brilliant female scientists all over the world!

A statue of Marie Curie stands in Warsaw, the capital city of Poland.

Today scientists at the Institut Curie in Paris continue Marie's work. They research new cancer treatments.

"Be less curious about people and more curious about ideas."

—Marie Curie

GLOSSARY

atom—the smallest particle of a substance that can exist

cancer—a disease caused by abnormal cells growing out of control

chemistry—the study of substances and their properties

doctorate—the highest degree awarded by a college or university

element—a natural substance that cannot be broken down into other substances

matter—anything that occupies space and has mass

physics—the study of matter and energy and their properties

pitchblende—a mineral that contains uranium and radium

radiation—energy traveling through space

radioactivity—the giving off of radiation

university—a high-level school in which students study for degrees and research is done

uranium—a radioactive element

X-ray—a form of energy that can pass through many materials

CRITICAL THINKING QUESTIONS

1. The text on page 6 says that in Marie's time, women in Poland were not allowed to go to college. How is this different from education today?

2. The text on page 10 describes how Marie met Pierre Curie. How did their meeting change her life?

3. How did Marie help soldiers during World War I?

READ MORE

Gordon, Fernando. *Marie Curie*. Scientists at Work. Minneapolis: Super Sandcastle, 2016.

Meltzer, Brad. *I Am Marie Curie*. Ordinary People Change the World. New York: Dial Books, 2019.

Sanchez Vergara, Isabel. *Marie Curie*. Little People, Big Dreams. New York: Lincoln Children's Books, 2017.

INTERNET SITES

Marie Curie the Scientist
www.mariecurie.org.uk/who/our-history/marie-curie-the-scientist

The Genius of Marie Curie
https://ed.ted.com/lessons/the-genius-of-marie-curie-shohini-ghose

INDEX